Layla's Life, My Words

An insight into the world of a child with foetal alcohol spectrum disorder (FASD)

ISBN: 978-1-716-41893-8

For my Arvind
who first introduced me to the SEN world.

ACKNOWLEDGEMENTS

I would like to acknowledge five professionals, who throughout our learning process, have been supportive and understanding to us as a family, and to Layla in particular; -

Valmerie Gordon
Occupational Therapist

Dr Mandy Bryon
Consultant Clinical Psychologist

Harriet Ostler
Clinical Nurse Specialist for Learning Disability

Dr Lara Shaffer
Consultant Paediatrician

Elenor Furze
SENCO

I would firstly like to thank Kirsten Elder who suggested my blogs should be turned into a book. Without her suggesting, the book would never have materialised. I am eternally grateful to Jonathan Dunlop, who agreed with Kirsten and also suggested who could help me with my project. This was the most useful suggestion as without it, I would have been stuck! A massive thank you to my friend Noro Napravnik, who I sent my blogs to via email (as he is not on social media) and who checked grammar and spelling without me even asking and sent them back before I posted them publicly. I never would have known where to start with this book, so a special thank you to my friend Shaun Hewitt, Layla's Shaun Taid, who supported me in every aspect of the book, giving me advice (whether asked for or not!), editing my drafts and suggesting content for the book. Thank you to Paul Donnelly for the technical work that neither Shaun nor I could manage in getting the book actually published. Thanks again to Noro, Shaun, Paul and mum for proof reading. And lastly but most importantly, a massive thank you to my family, I couldn't do this journey alone and of course, Layla, who has taught me so much.

CONTENTS

FOREWORD

An important lesson for all of us in schools – 'Happiness – it's the top of the pile really isn't it?'

Foetal Alcohol Spectrum Disorder is on the increase and can be 'hidden'. All of us in education need to be aware of the syndrome and how it affects children. We then need to understand how to work effectively with children with FASD to ensure that they flourish in our schools.

Layla's story is all too familiar. Schools are driven by a system that demands 'sameness' and yet we are all so different. This is especially true when children and young people are 'differently able'. The term disabled isn't helpful in education.

Being educated at home has made the world of difference to Layla but if you read this book as a leader in education, ask yourself 'Is it really too difficult to make the small changes that would let children like Layla thrive in our schools?'.

She had a package in place, but too often the package is 'hours of time' from a support assistant because that's easy to do and then 'something has been done'. What's really needed is to educate the adults in the school and then celebrate what children like Layla can do with the right support and understanding.

So Layla and her mum have found out almost by accident, that when she is encouraged and nurtured she begins to succeed and as we know 'success breeds success'.

Schools now more than ever need to change their approaches, listen to those who know the pupils well, stop doing what they've always done and listen to the child rather than the 'experts'.

As more families choose education at home while the system fails their children, this book needs to be read and acted upon by those who make decisions about provision and how schools are called to account. For too long they have perpetuated a Victorian system of factory sameness in education.

I wish Layla every success in her life as she discovers what she can do and isn't told what she can't do.

As Shushma says, '…then I remember my intentions are right, and my little girl is happy, and that's all that matters.'

Chris Britten, head teacher at Ysgol y Deri Special School
November 2020

INTRODUCTION

Covid-19 came unexpectedly, affecting everyone and changing the world forever. It is unprecedented, but it has also given me unprecedented opportunities. I was lucky when 'lockdown' came along, in that, I was safe in my home with my family, already working from home as we were already shielding Layla, my daughter. I made use of this opportunity, including writing this book, which I have wanted to do for a long while, but 'before' time was the biggest factor, originally my intention was to write a mini-series of blogs about my daughter. What I have come to realise, is that society has defined what a child or person with Special Educational Needs (SEN), or a disability looks or acts like, and that is not my daughter. I got frustrated trying to explain to professionals, friends and strangers that my daughter was not 'naughty' or 'disobedient', but had an invisible disability. I've even had someone tell me that Layla "Does not look disabled", and offered to show me people who *were* disabled. It is frustrating that even though I try and explain to people, they still don't 'get it'.

So, I decided to write the series of blogs to explain to my friends, what my daughter's invisible disability entails. I got a lot of positive comments on my posts, including the suggestion of compiling them into a short book and so this book was born. Thanks also to Shaun, a friend who is now family to me, who has helped me get this book together. Layla calls him, Shaun Taid, which is in Welsh means Grandad.

I hope that you, after reading this book, can pass on what you may learn, to that person in the supermarket who tuts at my daughter's behaviour, automatically believing that she is just spoilt or badly behaved, or those who make the snide remarks that I am a lazy mother who has yet to toilet train her daughter.

I also want to hopefully educate the professionals who have not yet heard of the diagnoses Layla has (surprisingly there are more than you would expect) and for them to be supportive to the families, as well as the child. Professionals often make the journey harder by not understanding what the child needs and therefore can't offer the right support, which then means, the families have to spend valuable time advocating, or being more vocal than they would like, to be heard for their child. This part of the SEN world is little known about to those outside of it, even though it is becoming more and more prevalent.

I also want this book to be a tool for parents whose children may have the same special educational needs as Layla, and for them to know that they are not alone – to show it *is* hard work *but* with strategies and love there is hope and beautiful moments. I have tried to be realistic and honest, I hope this comes across when you read the book.

Abbreviations the SEN parents live with every day . . .

ADHD – Attention Deficit Hyperactivity Disorder
CAFCASS – Child and Family Court Advisory and Social Services
EHCP* – Educational Health Care Plan
FASD – Foetal Alcohol Spectrum Disorder
LSA – Learning Support Assistant
OT – Occupational Therapist
PEG – Percutaneous Endoscopic Gastrostomy (feeding tube to the stomach)
SEN – Special Educational Needs
SIT – Sensory Integration Therapy
SPD – Sensory Processing Disorder

* Some children who have special educational needs have an educational health care plan, this is a legal document. The local authority allocates money to the school just for Layla, so that they can meet all the requirements mentioned in her EHCP. Layla has the highest band, band E, which means the school gets funding specifically for them to employ an learning support assistant, (usually called a one-to-one,) during school hours, just for Layla.

Part One – About us

Chapter 1 – An introduction to our family

I am Shushma, and I live with my parents, Mridula and Ashok and my older brother Nitin. I also had a younger brother Arvind who died in 2009, aged 13. He had Duchenne muscular dystrophy (DMD) and a mild learning disability. It was Arvind who introduced us to the world of special educational needs. Arvind attended a nursery in a special educational needs school (one of only two SEN primary schools in the local authority). Pupils who attend the school have severe learning difficulties and complex needs. One year I went in, to help at a Christmas party, after which I was asked if I would like to volunteer there, this then led to a job where I stayed for 19 years, first as a learning support assistant, then covering for teachers, later on teaching there myself.

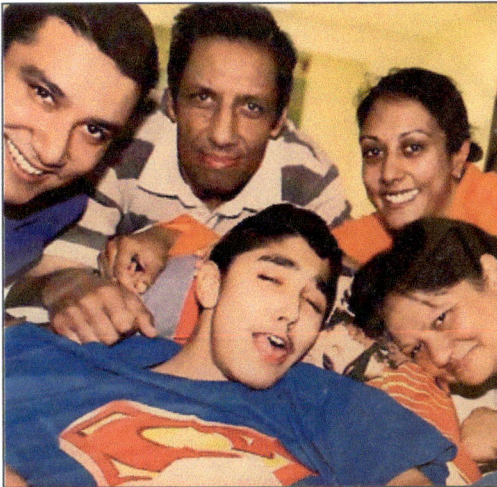

Nitin,
Ashok,
Shushma
Arvind and
Mridula

We are a very close family and support each other in everything we do. My mum had always wanted to try fostering when we were young, but as she was working and paying a mortgage, she felt it was best to wait. Then when I was 14 years old, Arvind was born, and then diagnosed with DMD when he was three. So again, mum felt it was best to wait as none of us could give our full support to an 'extra' child. Three years after Arvind died, my mum saw an advert in a local newspaper about a fostering information session, so thinking it was about time, myself and my dad went along with her. After hearing what was involved and as Dad was now retired and they had paid off their mortgage (mum was working but felt she wanted to give up her job for fostering), we decided as a family to offer ourselves for the assessment. My Dad is profoundly deaf, so we asked if I could be named as the second carer, which was agreed (even though our whole family is hands on involved with the extra childcare). We had an amazing social worker who did our assessment and we were approved in April 2013.

When we were going through our fostering assessment, my mum asked if only Asian children would be placed with us, as we would be happy to foster *any* child from *any* ethnicity. We were told, that in the past, if a child was placed with a carer of a different ethnicity, it was known as a 'bridging placement' and the child would only be with that carer, until a carer of the same ethnicity could be found. However, things had recently changed and local authorities were no longer allowed to use bridging placements, and now a child can, and will, be placed with a carer from a different ethnicity.

We had a few emergency placements of children needing temporary care; 'emergency' meaning we could get a phone call at any time, day or night to expect a child imminently, and the child could possibly stay a day, a month or years. Initially we only had children who stayed for a week at the most. After our care of Arvind, the fostering team felt we would be ideal to care for a child with special educational needs, but no child came along, until in August 2013 we received a phone call asking whether my mum could be on permanent standby for 'baby E' who was due to be born that October. No one was sure exactly when this baby would be born, whether they would have SEN, or even survive birth, due to the baby's birth mother drinking heavily during pregnancy. My mum said yes.

14

Chapter 2 – Fostering and adoption

From mid August, we were on standby in case 'baby E' was born early. We got a phone call on Friday the 18th of October 2013, to say that the mother had gone into labour, 'baby E' was born on Monday the 21st. We were finally allowed to bring her home when she was nine days old.

Layla's ethnicity is British white. When we got the placement information record (PIR), it mentioned that our placement with Layla was only temporary and was indeed a bridging placement, breaking their own rules. We were obviously upset, as we felt that we were only good enough when it suited social services because they had no one else. It would also be unsettling for Layla to go somewhere when she had got used to us. We disputed this with senior management, who agreed with us.

Even though she was born full-term, her weight was that of a premature baby. This meant my mum had to take Layla to the hospital nearly every week due to her poor weight as she was not drinking enough milk. She had also been born with two holes in the heart, a common 'side effect' when a pregnant mother drinks alcohol. She also had severe eczema which caused her hair to not grow.

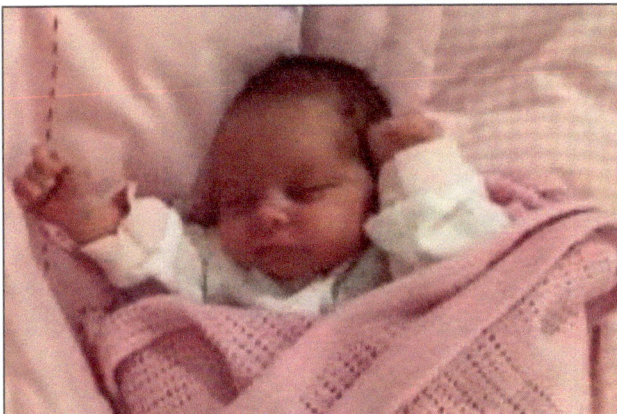

It was her birth parents who named Layla. I asked them during one of our contact sessions why that name – they said it was after their favourite song by Eric Clapton. Layla is also a popular name in India (spelt Laila in Arabic) and there are many Hindi songs for Laila. Layla gets so excited when she hears songs with her name.

For four months, Layla went through alcohol withdrawal symptoms, causing her to scream at high pitch, claw her face and not sleep during the day, or nights - all side-effects of withdrawal. When friends came over, they would say they would leave as she was so unsettled during that period. I was working full-time then, and we were all sleep deprived, as Layla would be up most of the night. It was my mum who would comfort her and support her through this time.

After three weeks of Layla being with us, we got a phone call from social services to say that we needed to take Layla to the hospital, as the results from her heel prick test (blood they take when babies are born to check for genetic illness) had come back saying Layla had Cystic Fibrosis. Layla was diagnosed on the 30th of November 2013.

During the next few months, Layla had several hospital admissions due to low fluid intake and chest infections, she always had a nasal feeding NG tube put in while admitted, to help hydrate her and she was also given prescribed milk that had all the nutrients and calories she needed to grow. She was also referred to the Gastro team who did several tests including an endoscopy and colonoscopy, which revealed she had duodenitis, inflammation of the small intestine. She was put on a strict diet and was not allowed wheat, eggs, dairy or soya. She was put on steroids, but the consultant was concerned of the long-term side effects, so was put on immune suppressant drugs which worked. Layla's two holes in the heart closed up naturally and the eczema cleared up after using several different creams on her body, which we still have to use daily.

In January 2014, we were told Layla was to be put forward for adoption, as her birth parents felt this was for the best. We discussed as a family what we all felt, and came to the conclusion, we all wanted Layla to be a permanent part of our family; so I would apply to adopt Layla, but we would bring her up together, which we still do, nearly seven years later.

When we heard that Layla was to be put forward for adoption, we asked her social worker and the recruitment team manager, whether being Asian would prevent us adopting her. The recruitment manager said this would not be an issue, but Layla's social worker didn't reply to my emails and she made no mention of it when we had face to face meetings. Fortunately, every child within the 'system' has a CAFCASS (child and family court advisory and social services) worker who is known as the child's guardian. At the final court hearing, we got a phone call from Layla's guardian, asking why we hadn't put our names forward for adopting Layla. When my mum explained the situation to her, the guardian said that Layla's social worker had not included our interest in her paperwork. (When asked about this, Layla's social worker said she forgot!.) The guardian came and visited us the same day and told us what we needed to do so we could start the assessment. If it was not for her, Layla would never have become part of our family.

I asked for the same social worker who did my foster carers assessment to do the adoption assessment, as she already knew everything about me. And on the 21st of July 2014, I was matched with Layla at panel. Matching means that during the assessment, the social worker felt I, as the adopter, would meet the unique needs of Layla. The next step was that the professionals read the assessment written by the social worker and then asked us any questions they may have, to reassure them that we are able to meet the unique needs of Layla.

It was during the assessment that foetal alcohol spectrum disorder was first mentioned. And like most people, we knew very little about FASD. My mum and I went several times to training sessions, but nothing prepares you for it, until you live with it, with the child. On the 12th of

December 2014, we went to the family court for a 'Celebration Hearing' which is what takes place after the court have granted the adoption order, and gives adoptive families a chance to celebrate the making of the order, to meet the judge and take photos, as well as receive the birth certificate.

Finally, Layla was officially my daughter and a legal part of our family.

During our training and adoption support group meetings, we were always advised by the local authority adoption team to be honest and open with Layla from the start, so that Layla would hear the word 'adoption' in ordinary conversation and start to ask questions as and when she was ready. I would then respond appropriately to her understanding. Someone from the adoption team, with my input, put together a 'Life Story' book of how and why Layla went into care with photos of her birth family. I used to read it to Layla when she asked questions, also, so that if a topic came up at school regarding families she wouldn't be confused. It is always readily available for her to look at it herself.

Part Two – Layla and her challenges

Chapter 3 – Foetal Alcohol Spectrum Disorder (FASD)

Even though I have worked in the special educational needs (SEN) field for 20 years now, once I entered the world of fostering, it opened up many more doors, additional insight into SEN, and things I had been completely oblivious to.

In society's eyes Layla seems 'ok', 'normal'. To me, her mum, of course, she is. Yet, every day is a challenge for Layla. As well as cystic fibrosis, Layla has foetal alcohol spectrum disorder (FASD), sensory processing disorder (SPD), a feeding tube (PEG), attention deficit hyperactivity disorder (ADHD), low muscle tone, hypermobility syndrome, hypoglycaemia, a learning disability as well as other things. Layla has also recently been assessed for autism, Let's be clear, I am not listing Layla's diagnoses for sympathy for Layla, or praise for ourselves, I am naming them to hopefully spread a little more awareness. Many people who do not have personal experience with the special educational need's world, perceive SEN to be a singular thing, i.e. a person in a wheelchair, who can't talk or understand you and is not toilet trained. That's how many people viewed Arvind, even though he was able to do the above.

So let's start with foetal alcohol spectrum disorder. Technically people with FASD are lifelong recovering addicts. This affects Layla's brain, as she has brain damage, due to her birth mother's drinking heavily throughout her pregnancy. Foetal damage from drinking alcohol is in most cases more severe than drug abuse during pregnancy. This means Layla will always have FASD, and, as she grows older, her 'issues' will become harder. Some statistics on it - 35% of adolescents who have FASD have had serious suicidal thoughts, whilst 13% make a serious attempt, contrasted with figures of 17% and 2% respectively in the general adolescent population (US National Library of Medicine), whilst many end up in the criminal system or homeless, because society does not see their disability, or understand it. However, with strategies and structure many are able to live a life that they want and follow their dreams.

Hardly anyone knows about FASD, yet it is the most common, non-genetic cause of learning disability in the UK (British Medical Association, 2007.) This condition is totally preventable, yet due to the taboo surrounding drinking alcohol whilst pregnant, it is hardly talked about. Now, the guidance recommends that no alcohol be consumed during pregnancy, or when planning a baby. However, some women may be drinking, not realising they are pregnant and by the time they do, it may be too late. Therefore it is important to raise awareness and to give prospective mothers as much information as possible, then they can make an informed choice. They must be supported, rather than have a stigma attached, both before the birth as well as after the birth of their child. I feel this information should be taught in secondary schools, as according to Professor Barry Carpenter, a lead researcher in the FASD field, when he lectures in schools a good 50% of teachers have not heard of it. He also suggests that FASD could affect as many as 1% of children in Western countries.

FASD means that Layla's receptive language is delayed. This is the ability to understand and process information. So Layla needs language broken down, be clear and concise. She takes things literally. She needs structure and routine to help with her anxiety, so that she knows what to expect and what is happening next. She needs visuals so she knows and understands things, such as how long she has to wait.

Layla forgets things, so in order to learn she needs repetition. Layla can talk well, but unfortunately, because of this people assume she knows what's been said. She can repeat 'the rules' but does not necessarily understand what they mean, and how they apply to her. I could tell her off for the same thing every day, but she won't learn, as she does not have that concept. Imagine when she's older and how society will deal with that.

Layla becomes agitated or anxious with change of routine, or unexpected changes. She is unable to name her emotions or how they make her feel.

People tell me I am lucky as she is such a sociable, confident child. She is not confident. She has no filter, no stranger danger awareness and will go with anyone, talk to anyone. She does not understand the consequences, obviously this will make her extremely vulnerable when she is older.

So this is when strategies come into place to help her in daily life. Some examples – every day we have to ask Layla what she wants for breakfast, even though it's the same things on offer, we have to name them. In the car, I have to ask Layla what she wants to listen to, even though it might be the same song we have been listening to on repeat for 3 months.

People assume she is being naughty, but actually, it's that she CAN'T, not that she WON'T!

This is not meant to sound negative, just realistic and so you can get an idea of what someone coping with FASD goes through on a daily basis, and also in order for you to appreciate how far Layla has already come.

Chapter 4 – The battle of getting an assessment of FASD

I learnt two years after Layla was born that social services should already have got the diagnosis of FASD for Layla, as only they had the necessary evidence to prove it (the birth mother's records). Without that evidence, doctors will not diagnose. I also found out after researching, that getting a diagnosis for Layla was going to be a battle. It took me another two years, advocating for Layla, before I finally got what we needed.

Why is this?

When a child is suspected of having FASD, you are referred to a geneticist. This part was plain sailing. The consultant did an assessment, took photos, could see some of the features in Layla that are typical of FASD. In Layla's case, a smaller than average head circumference, poor weight and height, thin upper lip and a flat nasal bridge to the nose, (many children don't have these features, as it depends when the alcohol was taken during the pregnancy). The geneticist said she would discuss with colleagues and see me again in 9 month's time!!! At the second appointment, I began to feel that I was being given the run around. This time she said I needed to obtain evidence that birth mother had been drinking. She also asked me what I was hoping to gain from a diagnosis, wasn't it labelling my child. She also said she didn't want to be sued by Layla when she was older. Yes, she really said that. I explained that having an official diagnosis of any child's

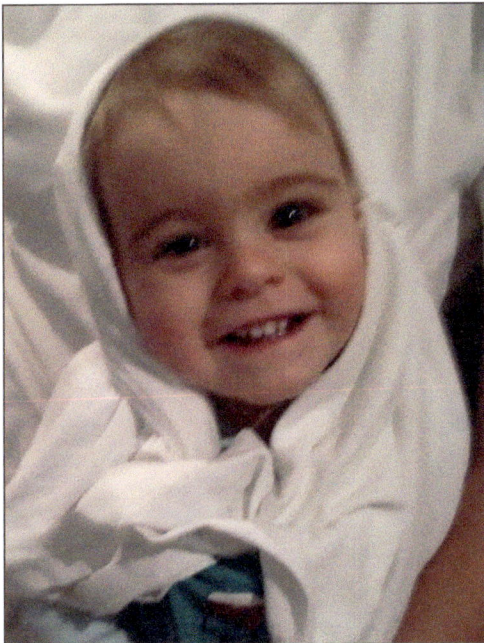

special needs opens doors at school, and she would be more likely to get the right support rather than be labelled as a 'naughty child'.

The doctor then said she would refer Layla to the Surrey clinic, who could do an assessment. I was upset, as I knew we would have to wait until Layla was six, as that is the criteria. The Surrey clinic is one of only two specialist centres that offer assessment for FASD, meaning waiting lists are long and if the Clinical Commissioning Group (CCG) refuse to pay (most do), families have to pay privately. After a lengthy battle I finally got confirmation that large amounts of alcohol had been consumed while Layla was a foetus, but the genetic consultant still refused to diagnose or refer.

The community paediatric consultant who Layla was under, went on training for FASD and came to understand why it is so important to diagnose, as well as *who* can diagnose. She could see I had been given the run around and having gone through this extra training realised that she herself could give the diagnosis. And so in mid January 2018, it was officially recognised that Layla had FASD and the search for 'solutions' could begin. I was so happy for Layla that she would now get the support she needed, and relieved that at least this battle had ended and positively.

I also feel that it is important for Layla herself to understand, that the way she sometimes behaves is not her fault. Right from when Layla was in reception class, it started to dawn on her that she was different to her peers and she would ask questions; "Why don't I eat at school?" "Why can't I do the same work as other children?" "Why do I have a feeding tube?" and "Why do hairbands and clips irritate me?" As with questions about her adoption, we have been completely open with Layla answering these questions, hopefully in language she can grasp. I have told Layla why she was in care and why she feels 'different'. I've also bought books, including one written by Helen Simpson, an adult who has FASD, called 'The Way I Am Is Different'. It's a children's book about a boy with foetal alcohol spectrum disorder.

Chapter 5 – Sensory Processing Disorder (SPD)

Simply put, SPD is when a child has a difficult time receiving and responding to information from their senses. Children who have sensory issues may have an aversion to anything that triggers their senses, including the five 'common' senses; sight (light), sound, touch, taste or smell. There are however, three more senses-

- Proprioception – This is the internal awareness we have for our body. It's what helps us maintain posture and bodily control. It's also what tells us about how we're moving and occupying the space we are in.
- Vestibular – This is our spatial recognition, controlled by the inner ear. It's what keeps us balanced and coordinated.
- Interoception – This is the sense of what's happening *in* our body. Basically, it's how we feel. This includes whether we feel hot or cold, and whether we feel emotions.

Sensory processing tells us when we need the bathroom, where our body is in relation to our surroundings, even which way up we are. Imagine hanging upside down but your senses don't tell you that you are upside

down. Think about holding a pencil, but not being able to feel how much pressure you need to hold it. These are some of the things that children that have sensory processing disorder have to deal with.

In order to help Layla, we take her once a week for sensory integration therapy, which is a form of occupational therapy that uses fun, play-based sensory activities (rotary swinging, climbing a rock wall, finding toys hidden in a ball pit, jumping on a trampoline while trying to catch a ball etc.). This helps her brain respond to sensations and movement in a more 'organised' way.

Over time, with repetitive exposure to sensory activities (which become increasingly more challenging), Layla's brain will start to integrate sensory input more efficiently. She will better self-regulate (fewer meltdowns), be more focused, have less anxiety and she will feel more comfortable and confident in her own skin – but only if we follow *exactly* the sensory diet program that was set out by the occupational therapist, daily, making sure the environment is the same as well as the routine.

A sensory diet is a program of sensory activities Layla does during the day with us to ensure she is getting the input her body needs. A sensory activity may be spinning 10 times to the left and then spinning 10 times to the right.

A small insight in how SPD affects Layla. Layla's shoes have to be slip on, no Velcro, no laces or buckles, as this becomes a sensory overload for Layla. If she has Velcro, laces or buckles she will keep tightening them to get pressure on her feet. The same applies for clips, hairbands, baseball caps, helmets etc.

When going to a place such as a shopping centre, it's a sensory overload; people, noise, lights etc., and so she loses focus, gets over excited and anxious. The result is, that Layla seeks out 'normality' in movement, such as jumping, bumping and crashing, as well as sensory input, by mouthing things, such the handrail of the escalator due to the vibration, or putting her hands down the side of cold fridges in the frozen aisles, so her hands freeze and then running off. One of the more concerning 'mouthing' actions is when Layla mouths chewing gum pulled from under a table or till!

She has no awareness of the personal space of others and will often give bear hugs, which in reality are squeezes so hard they hurt!

Layla has low muscle tone and hypermobility, which means her joints are more 'bendy' than yours or mine and they often ache. She tires easily and becomes lethargic. It also means she can hurt herself easily. Hence why she has a wheelchair, *but* she also gets hyper and pushes herself beyond her limits as she does not know when to stop, then comes the irritability and tantrums as she can't identify the feeling of exhaustion. She also has poor balance and trips up over 'thin air'. She has to look at her feet when doing any physical movement such as running or climbing on equipment as she can't co-ordinate.

Layla has difficulty with extreme temperatures, so would not wear a coat, a hat, or tights in winter as she has not worn them in summer. She still has to have a hot shower in the summer. Her food has to be cold, not even warm. She is unable to regulate when she is thirsty or hungry, but that's for another chapter. We are working on strategies so that Layla can identify when she is dysregulated and can ask for things, such as her weighted blanket, or the MP3 player so she can self regulate, burning off that sensory overload. This will mean that when Layla takes exercise, such as playing on her scooter, she will realise when to stop and can ask to go on my shoulders when she is tired, coming home whilst listening to music.

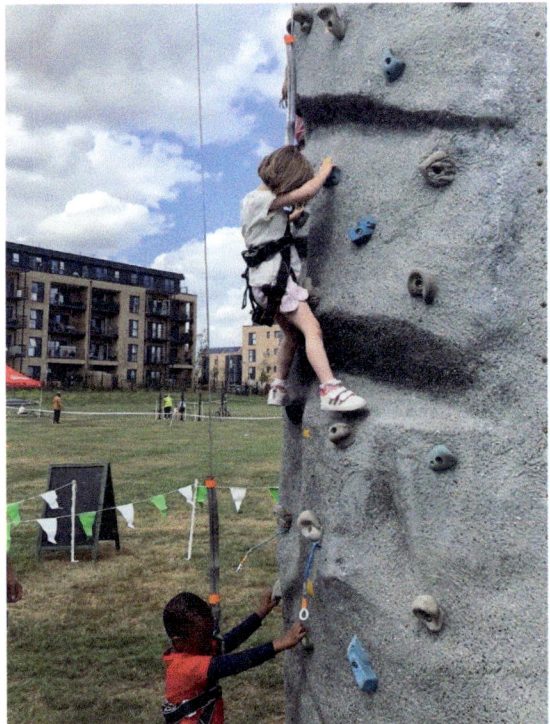

Chapter 6 – Eating and the feeding tube, known as the PEG

This chapter is about something very close to my heart, so I really want to explain it to people. We all probably assume that when someone can't eat orally, that there is some physical reason why they can't, which is why many friends and professionals don't understand why Layla doesn't eat.

I've had well-meaning friends says to me – "Why does she have a PEG when she can eat?" or "Are you not worried she is not eating?" or "Is she a fussy eater?"

Professionals – "She will copy the other children at school" and "She will eat when she is hungry".

NO! NO! NO! NO! NO! NO! NO! NO! NO!

When Layla was born her weight was that of a premature baby, even though she came at 40 weeks. Each week we had to take her to hospital as her weight was so low - they call it failure to thrive. I hate that 'diagnosis' (terminology) but still, they list it under that title. This is a common side-effect of FASD, not eating and poor weight gain. Hence why Layla had a PEG at 20 months old, but not without a fight.

Layla has mild aspiration, not enough to warrant a PEG in a child with no other health issues, but that PEG is now our lifesaver, with hardly any hospital admissions due to not eating since it was fitted.

Layla can't regulate when she is hungry or thirsty due to SPD. She has appetite control difficulties as well as oral-motor delay. This means that the muscles in her mouth are delayed and she has trouble co-ordinating her lips, tongue and jaw muscles due to her brain not sending the right signals to the mouth muscles. So Layla eats slowly and has trouble chewing food such as meat and therefore won't eat it. A child with oral-motor disorder may also have trouble talking. Happily, Layla has no trouble with talking, except when to stop sometimes!

So, what does this mean. We have made huge progress since she was a baby. She hardly ate and what she did eat was limited. She could never eat wet things such as sauces or milk in her cereal. Now she does both. She would have a meltdown if food got around her mouth Nowadays though Layla *will* eat but only at home. Due to her SPD, the outside world is overwhelming, and so her brain has to manage that so forget eating as that's not important. It's flight or fight. This means she does not eat when we go out, or on holiday or at school. (So much for the professional's advice that she will copy other children!)

When she is at school, she does not eat from 6.00 am, when she has her breakfast, until 5.00 pm when she gets home. On two days a week I pick her up early, but because I usually pick her up early for a reason, such as swimming, she still can't eat, as her brain tells her "Mummy has picked me up to swim, so swim then eat". This means that the school has to use the feeding tube, but as Layla's tummy is small, the prescribed 'milk' she has, can only be given a small quantity at a time.

As Layla will throw up if her food is injected through her PEG too quickly, for the ease of the school, a mechanical pump is attached which slowly and continuously delivers the nutrient. This means that Layla is on her PEG continuously whilst in classes, being detached from it only when she is outdoors or during physical activities. Then, when she comes home, we're lucky if she will eat a small half a Jacket potato (plain with nothing added) because she is so dysregulated. Layla does not consume sufficient calories orally, so at times she has a hypoglycaemia where her blood sugars can fall dangerously low. So, on top of everything else, we also have the blood sugar monitor to check her levels if we think she is having a 'hypo' so we can intervene. But this is now managed much more easily due to regular use of the PEG. Layla doesn't eat huge amounts, but what she does eat, and the widening variety she will now try brings me such joy.

Using the automatic feeding pump was never ideal at school. Layla needs to be watched closely so that she doesn't pull on it which can have serious consequences. That didn't always happen.

In consequence of her SPD, she happily eats plain toast and never bothers us for junk food (her favourite food is fruit). In addition, she rarely drinks orally, so daily we have to get 700mls of water through her PEG so she is hydrated, as with cystic fibrosis (CF) (I haven't even mentioned that yet!) you sweat more and so lose salt. Being well hydrated also helps to keep her bowels moving, as again that is another thing related to CF. We are constantly persuading Layla to eat as many calories as she can, as people with CF can't absorb their fat intake properly, or adequately digest food. Layla is also given 60ml of water every hour through her PEG – any more, and she throws up, as her stomach can't take the volume. Trust me, I've learnt this the hard way!

Layla does not eat with us, at the same time as us, or at the dinner table. It's too busy and overwhelming. Often, she sits on Nani's or my lap to eat (attachment issues due to the neglect of her birth mother) or next to one of us on the sofa where she feels safe. She has a divider plate, so she can clearly see her food and the quantity and knows what is expected of her. Depending on how she is feeling, either she will ask myself or Nani to feed her. Increasingly she will feed herself, though she can only manage using a spoon at present. One strategy we have found, is sitting Layla at a small plain white table with no distractions. It can take up to an hour, and no rushing either. We can't leave her, otherwise she will walk off as the food doesn't interest her, or she loses focus if we are not there, reminding and prompting her to eat. This does mean one of us gets to sit down for an hour!

If we have friends for lunch, we don't tell Layla, otherwise she won't eat; she will be too excited, so she eats before they come. If we are going somewhere, even a children's birthday party, we try and get Layla to eat at home first.

All this means, that when we walk through the door at home after being out, Layla will have a meltdown. Her brain tells her that she is hungry, as she is in her safe place, but most of the time Layla can't identity what that feeling it is. When you see Layla with food in a photo, most of the time she has not eaten it, or only had a few spoonsful. But, and this is one of Layla's own strategies, if someone asks what she has eaten, because she knows what society expects of her, she will repeat the lunch other children have had at school as she knows that's what people want to hear. This also avoids the follow on questions, of 'Why don't you eat?' etc. etc. etc. . . . but, Layla has made HUGE progress with her eating, and if I could express one thing for people to remember, both for Layla and for other SEN children, it is again, CAN'T, not WON'T.

Chapter 7 – Attachment issues

When we first decided to foster as a family 8 years ago, just like most of society, we thought all these children need, is a loving home and they will be 'fine', 'fixed'. How wrong were we. There *is* no magic wand we can use, just resilience, empathy, love, emotional upheaval and an abundance of patience!!!!

Both my mum and I did a 3 months attachment course, and boy, did it teach us how to think differently. You don't parent the 'normal' way, (or the way most of us would understand as 'normal') due to child's trauma or neglect, which often affects the wiring of the brain of the more vulnerable children who are fostered, this can cause attachment issues with the children.

Layla was already with us when we had another foster child placed with us, and through that child we learnt pretty quickly what attachment difficulties were and it was a lived-in experience for five years for us all. I now understand why some adults who were abused when they were a child, abuse children/adults themselves (not that it makes it right). And when well-meaning people say it's ok, you have had them since they were a baby or at a young age they will be ok, that makes no difference, except the severity maybe, even as a foetus babies are subjected to drugs/alcohol, their mother's stress levels and they hear raised voices and arguments.

What is attachment?
Attachment is about our need to feel loved, safe and protected in our relationships. This begins when we are a foetus in the womb and when we are born. Most of us will receive love, security and attention from our parents/caregivers consistently as babies, as they provide for our needs of hunger, cold, fear and pain. This means the foundation of the brain will be wired healthily as the child develops secure attachments. When babies don't form a secure attachment due to neglect or abuse, this causes the brain to be wired differently and they may become

traumatised and learn not to trust adults. This in turn may lead to self-regulating problems and anxiety.

With Layla, how does this present itself?
Before birth, Layla was subjected to drugs and alcohol, hearing arguments and the physical abuse of her mother. For nine days, immediately after her birth she had constantly changing nurses and two different hospitals settings to contend with. Babies don't remember right? Subconsciously they clearly do. When they cry, due to hunger, cold or fear etc. and this need is not met, this inevitably leads to attachment difficulties which affect them for the rest of their lives; as their brain develops, the baby soon learns that they can only rely on themselves; they can't trust any one person to meet their needs. One simple instance I've noticed with children with attachment difficulties. If today, the teacher said "Hi" and asks how the child is in class and then tomorrow they don't, we rationalise it; they were busy, distracted, but the child can't. To them it's "They don't care about me, they are pretending to care".

A good example of how babies absorb everything. Layla, even today, will not go anywhere without my mum, as in go on holiday or a hospital admission and only sleeps when my mum is there. Why? Because during that first 10 months when we were fostering Layla, I was working full time. We also at that time didn't know how long she would be with us, and whether at some point she would go on for adoption. So when Layla was going through alcohol withdrawal symptoms (for four months), screaming, high-pitched screaming, day and night whilst clawing her face, it was my mum who was supporting her through it, 24/7, so Layla knows the smell and touch of my mum. People ask me "Does that not upset you?" The answer is no. Why should it. I understand why. I am also secure in the relationship I have with Layla. She loves me and knows I am her mum. Layla still can't sleep by herself due to her attachment difficulties, she is still on some level, scared of us leaving her.

I mentioned that we have to parent differently. For example, if Layla were to break something on purpose, because I said no to something she wanted to do, (which doesn't happen often,) it wouldn't be any use yelling and issuing a punishment or consequence. It will be looking at the behaviour. So it would be better to say, "I can see you didn't like me saying no to you, as it made you feel angry (acknowledging the feelings). What was it that made you feel like that?" Hopefully, Layla will find words to at least express some of what she is feeling and I can explain why I said no. We then clear up any mess together, so we reconnect and attune our relationship. This may not happen right away, as Layla will be too upset to regulate or rationalise, so it may be a few hours later or even the next day.

So why wouldn't I shout or give a consequence?
Because I would be re-affirming her unconscious belief that no one loves her, that she is horrible. This could impact on her self-worth, arising from us unintentionally making her feel guilty or ashamed.

Also as Layla grows, those feelings of low self-worth may become huge and manifest as she lives with the belief that "My own birth parents didn't love me enough to keep me" and so that's rejection and this plays a major part of her wanting to fit in, especially with peers, even if it is the 'wrong' ones as, at least they care and love her, rather than not at all. This makes them so vulnerable.

What I have learnt from all this is, CHOOSE YOUR BATTLES (so hard to do though!)

As Pam Leo (author of the book 'Connected Parenting') says "How we treat the child, the child will treat the world".

Chapter 8 - Cystic Fibrosis (CF)

A positive from Covid-19 is that it has created some awareness of CF. So many people have said to me, when I explain what CF is, "Oh but she looks alright". So what is CF? It is a condition that causes mucus to build up in the lungs and digestive system. This causes lung infections and problems with digesting food. In the 1960s, children were lucky to live past their fifth birthday. Since then, half of people living with CF will live to celebrate their 46th birthday. So how does CF affect Layla. Well I say that Layla is 'lucky' as her CF is classed as mild compared to other children, and has only had three admissions for intravenous antibiotics for lung infections (administered by a 'central line', which is a catheter placed in a large vein in the neck or heart. Something that is common in CF). She is pancreatic sufficient, so has the pancreatic enzymes required to digest food. However, I know this could change as she gets older or if she gets a serious chest infection. At the moment, oral antibiotics work, but she is usually on them a month at a time and she will get four or five chest infections a year. The side effects of the antibiotics usually means she get diarrhoea, thrush and/or is sensitive to the sun depending which one she has to take.

With Covid-19 the symptoms usually start with a dry cough, but then becomes productive or wet, known to us as chesty. This is what happens to Layla with CF. She may be well in herself, or look well but when her cough becomes productive, I have to do a cough swab (how they are testing Covid-19) and send it to Layla's CF team. They then check it and ring me to let me know what bug is growing in Layla's lungs to cause the mucus and will then identify an antibiotic that will target that particular bug. The antibiotics are always a two-week course. The cough is not infectious to you or me, but for Layla antibiotics are to stop the scaring of the lungs, so that hopefully she won't need a lung transplant when she is older, and to shift the mucus sitting on the lungs. She also has to do a cough swab every time she has a CF appointment.

There are bugs in the environment (Pseudomonas for example) that can cause very difficult infections for people with CF – these bugs live in damp, rotting vegetation or stagnant water.

This means that Layla has not been allowed to play in the water tray or mud kitchen at school, visit a farm nor use a public swimming pool. The amount of people that ask Layla if she has enjoyed going swimming on holiday, or the new swimming pool at Butlins (one of Layla's favourite places). Everything has to be sterile for Layla, at school as well as at home, so like with Covid-19, clean, clean, clean. It also means I don't let her go out when it freezing cold, damp or raining, due to it affecting her lungs, *or* when it is boiling hot; people with CF sweat more than people who don't have CF.

There isn't a cure for CF. Treatment for Layla is physiotherapy to clear her airways, at least twice a day, more if she has a wet cough and this usually means using her acapella machine (this is a hand-held device which helps to clear mucus and expand the lung. Layla calls this her 'butterfly'). Another physiotherapy is blowing a volcano of bubbles out of a bottle from the suction tube she blows into, making a whole heap of wet mess but fun too. She has to do this 10 times, 10 sets. After 10 times, she has to huff and then cough. It also means staying as active as possible, so no worry there then! She takes her nebuliser twice a day which she dislikes with a passion, due to the rubber texture around her mouth and nose, as well as the noise from the machine. Layla also takes daily medication, which she can now name!

Layla needs a diet that is higher in calories and fat than other people, due to the difficulty she has digesting food. So the usual healthy eating guidelines do not apply to her, and eating food like chocolate or things with loads of salt, is part of her treatment plan to make sure she gets the calories she need. Fat chance! Her idea of a meal is watermelon or Weetabix!!!

People with cystic fibrosis can't mix with other people who have the condition, this is additionally isolating, as they can't meet up, in support groups for instance. They carry bugs in their lungs that wouldn't be harmful to those without the condition, but can be to others with CF. This means that whenever she has an appointment at her hospital, we have to wait at reception before being ushered into a room, so Layla is not lining up with other children who have CF, or its stay six feet part and then we have to stay there until our appointment has finished.

What does the appointment consist of? We have to see a range of professionals; the doctor, the physio, who does the cough swab and checks on her physio routine, the lung respiratory staff, who do the lung function test, the CF specialist nurse, the psychologist to see how we are all coping, the dietician who plots Layla's height and weight, and they tell us if they are happy with it, and what changes need to be made to her diet.

The professionals are all under the CF team. Layla has to have an annual review which is her MOT and they also do a bladder scan and X-ray of chest, bloods, pooh sample etc. to make sure all is well. When she has been admitted into hospital, Layla always has her own en suite as she is not allowed to leave her room and it means, that everyone who comes in wears a mask, apron and gloves so not to pass anything on to Layla.

Once Layla turned five years old, she was allowed to join Nuffield gym, as they are a health charity and work in partnership with CF centres, where she has her own personal trainer who has a session with her once a week. The looks I got at first from other gym members! Layla loves it there and it is part of her physio. I can also take her swimming there, which I do once a week also as part of her physio treatment.

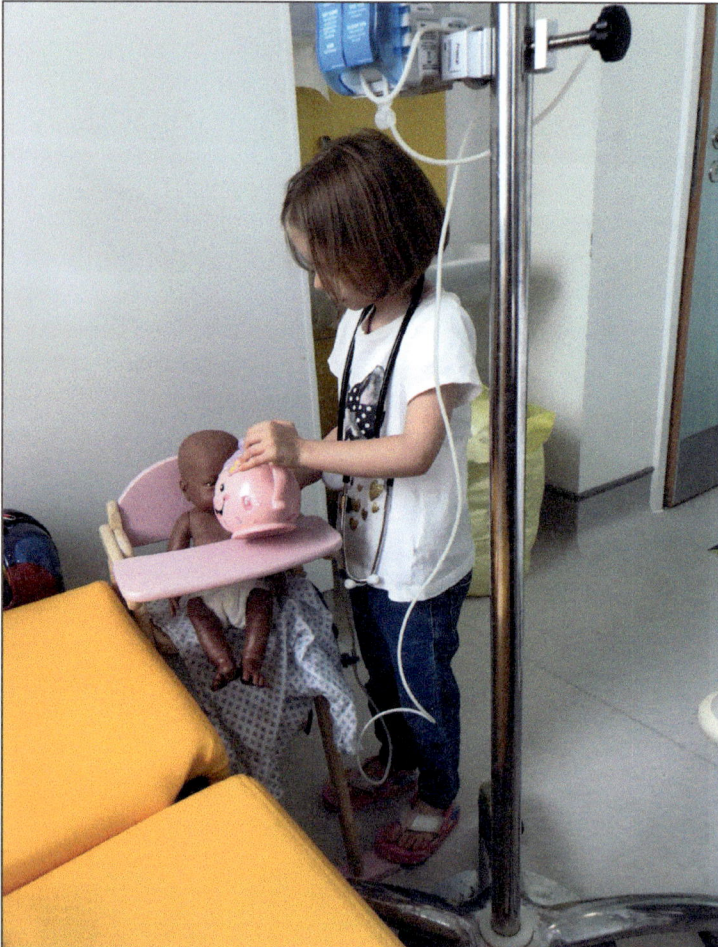

Chapter 9 – Learning Disability

People often confuse a learning difficulty with a learning disability. I was one of them.

A learning *difficulty,* is a condition which creates an obstacle to a specific form of learning, like dyslexia and reading; this only impacts a certain area of a person's IQ (intelligence quotient).

Layla has a learning *disability.* A learning disability is a reduced intellectual ability and difficulty with everyday activities – for example in Layla's case, socialising, age-related tasks (which will take her longer to learn) and the need for added support to develop new skills and understand complicated information. Hence why she has a one-to-one learning support assistant (LSA) full-time at school and an Educational Health Care Plan (EHCP) which is reviewed each year. For example, she is in year 1, and while she can count to 30, she does not know what numbers mean or the quantity, but the year group have moved on to number bonds. To you and me that's 2 different numbers that add up to another number. For example, 5 + 3 = 8. If I show her three teddies and ask how many more teddies do I need to make 8, she wouldn't know. And if I show her the five teddies and say see 3 + 5 is 8 teddies, she just sees 8 teddies. She does not understand the concept. Yet.

I have had success teaching Layla about halves and whole during lockdown by using peanuts! So, I showed her one half of a peanut and another half of a peanut and then put them together so it's a whole. It's thinking outside the box and being creative and real.

Layla's learning disability affects all aspects of her life, such as crossing the road. She knows cars come and it is dangerous, yet she will still step out on the road without checking to see it is clear. Another, funnier example is, that Layla likes to play 'Hide and Seek', daily. Yet Layla still hides in the same place each time and still finds it fun and hilarious when either Nani or I look high and low for her, then say "Found you" at the end. For Layla she is going back to the first place she had hidden the first time we played it. She does not understand that she can hide in a different place each time. Yep, she takes things literally. This is a learning disability.

This means that Layla finds it hard to learn things the first time. She needs time to learn a new skill and understand it. She learns through repetition and visually. Hence why Nani has been teaching her how to cook during Covi-19. She loves it. It's regulating, it's simplified to tailor around Layla's needs and repetitive. She is learning about Maths as she weighs things and learning about spices and names of utensils and food. This is a life skill that will be so much more important to her in her adult life than learning algebra or a times table.

She needs people around her who have patience, believe in her, and, guess what, if she can't do it, to say it's okay, because none of us can do everything. It knocks Layla's confidence when she is unable to learn something and she gets frustrated, but it's up to us to recognise the signs and interject and adapt teaching to suit her. If she is getting frustrated, it's not her, it's us. We either have not explained it to her to suit her understanding, or we are expecting too much, so setting her up to fail.

Yet play a song she likes, and she will memorise the words within a day! So, it's about tapping into things of interest to her.

So, today, we learnt about symbolic items that represent countries; Ireland, the green shamrock and Irish dancing; Scotland, the bagpipes and kilts, all by watching songs from Indian films. I think that's why, seeing her confidence grow whilst I taught her how to play tennis during 'lockdown' was amazing.

Yet society sees Layla as a capable young girl. She is, but not to the level they want, and when she says "No" or the 'bad' behaviour starts, they see it as a 'cop out' rather than seeing it as her saying, "I can't do this as it's too hard, but I don't feel confident telling you that, in case you think I am stupid".

We want Layla to learn life skills that will help her in her adult life. She now knows the difference between a pound coin and a two-pound coin. We bought a piggy box with her name on it and my mum 'rewards' her for certain things, things she won't fail at, such as listening to mummy when you are on your scooter. This way it's seen as a positive and we can build on it and say, well if you do *this*, such as waiting until a timer finishes, you can get a pound. This encourages positive behaviour. The downside *for us* is that Layla will now say "If I do this, may I have a pound?" She doesn't understand the importance of money yet, or that she can spend it on things. For Layla, the action of putting the coin in the box and the sound the money makes when she shakes it is the fun part.

My heart swells with pride now, when Layla shows she sees home as a

safe haven. A space where she can say, "Mummy, I don't understand what you are saying", or "Slow down, you are going too fast". It reminds me to check the language I use, or how I am showing Layla how to do something. It's not her that needs to adapt, but me. Just like the hide and seek game.

Layla being able to tolerate a helmet is yet another small victory.

Chapter 10 – Anxiety

Layla has anxiety. "What does a child have, to be anxious about?" I often hear.

What I have realised is that I can't eliminate Layla's anxiety, but I can help her to manage it by pointing out or naming it in a positive way. By me saying that she seems to be anxious, she is becoming aware of situations, or people, that make her anxious, and we can build up a strategy that will help her during that time. For example, I will say, "Layla I can see you may be anxious right now as you are pulling your skin and you only seem to do this when you're anxious". Layla used to say "No I am not", but over time she come to recognise it and will say "I am anxious", then we can talk about why. For instance, this could be when she has to have a hospital mask on her face for her yearly lung function test. I validate her feeling by saying, "I know you don't like the mask and it is really not nice having something over your face like that, but I am sorry, it's important you have it. You can sit on mummy's lap and squeeze my hand and Nani and I will be there". I also made a visual timetable so that Layla will know how many times they will make her wear the mask and make sure the lung specialist sticks to it. By doing all of this, I am not dismissing her fears, but nor am I amplifying them. I want Layla to understand what she is anxious about, and to let her know, that I know she is scared, and that it's okay to have those feelings, but I'm here for her, to help her get through it.

I will explain this every time we go for an appointment, but each time, the 'I know best' professional think they know my child better than me! They show this by saying things like, "We'll get the play therapist to read a book or blow bubbles to take her mind off it and tell her not to look when they are taking blood". Arrgghh excuse me, you are not listening... Well I don't say this out loud of course and I might swear under my breath, but what I do say is, "I'm really sorry, but with Layla the quicker it's done, the better, as she will have less time to become anxious".

By doing this, I am keeping the anticipatory period short. This works so much better. We found this out the hard way. If I know Layla is going to be anxious about something, we don't tell her until the day and probably an hour before otherwise she can't sleep, she won't eat and until it happens, she will be worked up about it. Her anxiety could be skin picking, subtle hair pulling, picking her scabs, sweating, crying etc. By telling Layla only an hour before, she doesn't have as much time to be anxious, it also gives her time to ask questions. Also, if I have the symbols, I use a visual timetable.

I really dislike the changing of the clocks. Well that's what I call it when we put the clocks an hour forward or backwards.
In summer Layla can't sleep as in her head, you don't sleep unless it is dark outside!

Layla does not like the dark. We don't know why, but my assumption is that subconsciously she remembers what happened when she was born, and it has had a lasting effect. I say this because I will never forget when she was nine days old; walking into the hospital bay, there was Layla on her own, in the dark, awake, wearing only a baby vest and a hospital blanket wrapped around her. She was awake, but lying still, it was about 7.30 in the evening. How must she have felt at nine days old when she had been inside a womb for the past 9 months.

When the clocks go back in winter, it gets darker quickly and so this causes Layla to be anxious. When we go to hospital, we are there all day and so it's dark by the time we leave and Layla used to get worked up about going home in the dark, as she can't see in the car and so she does not know what is happening and if it is safe. I remember her looking out of the window and getting anxious that it was getting dark, while we waited in the room to be seen by the different professionals. I then had a brainwave, "Layla, there are some beautiful things that happen in the dark. Can you guess?" Layla said "No". Well, the moon and the stars come out at night and the sky looks beautiful. That can be our light. When we walk to the car, let's see if we can find the moon and see if it can follow us home". Now Layla loves to look out for the moon.

Another reason that causes anxiety, is if I have to take a different route going to school or going home, due to traffic or a diversion. She worries she will be late to school and will say, "Oh no, oh no. We are going to be late", or "Do you know where you are going? We are going to get home, aren't we?" So what I do here, is think of things with Layla about what will happen if we get to school late (not that we ever have been, as we are always super early) and Layla will go through the scenario, and usually I say, "Well that's not so bad is it? As long as we get there". I sometimes pose the question, "What could we do if we got lost?" so Layla knows what we would do if we did.

Layla gets anxious when she hears unexpected or unfamiliar noises, if her one-to-one assistant is not there at school, or if she has watched or read something such as 'The Three Little Pigs', where Layla thinks the wolf may eat her up, this really worries her, so of course, we have to be careful what she watches or reads, as she won't sleep.

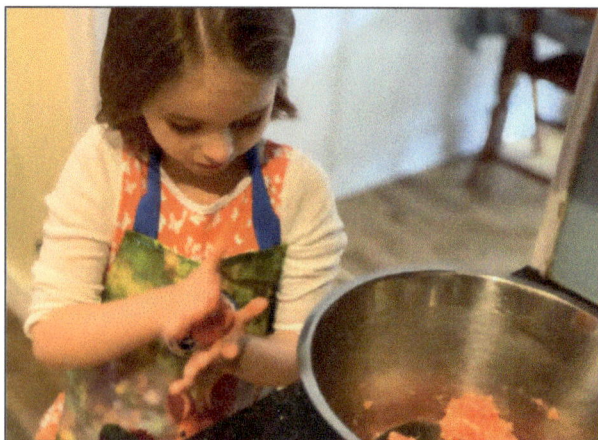

A couple of times a week I upload photos and video clips to Facebook of Layla cooking. 'Chef Layla'! Yesterday I also uploaded bloopers of her laughing (with Layla's permission), which of course, anyone who knows Layla will love. But I don't do this very often as Layla insists on getting it right; it causes her anxiety about what people will think if she does it 'wrong'. This comes from her experiences at school. Both from peers, friends and professionals alike, and the expectations they demand of her. To some extent the subtle bullying by a few children hasn't helped either. This is not malicious bullying, but as Layla is increasingly not at the same level of learning as the rest of the class and is not yet toilet trained, it is noticed and commented on. Layla is aware that she is different, and this just goes to reinforce it.

What has really worked is making her shapes (from Mister Maker), her worry thoughts. For those that do not watch CBeebies, shapes are just that – shapes. Mister Maker is a guy who does arts and crafts and he has shapes, the triangle, circle, square and rectangle. I bought them as teddies with a zip at the back to put things in. This is great as Layla will write her worry (we do this for her) and she chooses her shape and puts

it in the back and closes the zip, then the next morning she checks, and her worry has gone as the shape has eaten her worry. I tell you it's a nightmare remembering to throw that paper away when she has gone to bed and which of the shapes it's in. We have come so close, several times, when Layla goes to her shape!!! The stunts I have had to pull off!!! Originally, we did it with Layla each night but now when Layla has a worry, she will come to us and say I need to write my worry down.

Part Three – Home-education

Chapter 11 – The decision to home-educate

So, what was supposed to be a one-off Facebook post to friends about why I was thinking of home-educating Layla, has turned into a book!

Why? I realised after doing research into home-education, that most of us are unaware of what it really is, or what it involves. And because most of my friends only see snippets and partial aspects of Layla's world, on social media or face to face, they may not understand why I was considering it, unless I explained Layla's world fully. So it ended up being a series of blogs about Layla's life, before I could even get to home-education.

First a bit on home education.
So why do I say home-education rather than home-schooling. I promise it's not me being snobby. When I am interested in something, I become a geek and have to research all about it, be it home-education or some celebrity!
Home-schooling means teaching the national curriculum at home and having 'targets' throughout the school year, based on the year group a child is in.
Home-education means that the education a parent/carer will give will be tailored around their child's specific needs, and contrary to beliefs, while education between the ages of five and 16 is compulsory in the UK, school is not. Home-education also means there is no legal requirement to have a timetable, or to stick to national term dates. So, it will also be possible to take Layla away for breaks, during 'term time'. Meaning that places such as Butlins, or North Wales (her favourite places) will not be as busy, so sensory overload can hopefully be kept to the minimum. More about breaks later.

A recent study by the education publication 'Schools Week', mentioned that the number of children being home schooled, has almost doubled in the past six years in the UK (as of 2020). I can see why now. If I am honest, I probably wouldn't have understood before, why a parent or carer would choose it, or, just how easy the procedure is!

Lockdown has suited Layla perfectly, as even though we kept a structure and routine, we didn't have a ridged timetable. We were flexible. I didn't do any of the work the school sent for Layla's year, instead, I searched online for websites that have free resources, such as BBC Bitesize, as well as using my own common sense, to adapt information for Layla as well as tapping into her interests. Layla was not confined to a classroom having to learn what the government thinks all children *should* learn. I would plan the week in advance with my mum so I can be organised with the tools I need. Of course, things haven't always gone to plan, due to work, appointments (all via Zoom) or because Layla couldn't regulate. But that's ok as we are flexible. Sometimes learning is impromptu, which is the best learning at times and heart-warming. We are also learning all the time from the world around us. For example, coming back from her scooter ride recently, Layla saw some beautiful sunflowers with bees collecting pollen. I spoke about how they are making honey back at their hive. She loved learning about this and was proud when we passed them again the next day, to recite the 'lesson' back to me as she had remembered it.

Layla needed a movement break every 10 minutes at school as her concentration levels are shorter than her peers. The work the school set, should have been tailored for Layla, but it was not, so Layla struggled with it. She didn't enjoy her time in year one. Whilst there, she started to realise that she was different to her peers.

Layla had a full time LSA (learning support assistant) whilst at school who is funded through Layla's educational health care plan. Some children who have special educational needs have an EHCP, this is a legal document outlining the needs of a child. The local authority allocates money to the school just for Layla so they can meet all the requirements mentioned in the EHCP. Layla has the highest band, which means, the school get funding to employ a support assistant just for Layla. Her LSA had to take her outside the classroom to do her work, as when the other children saw the one-to-one helping Layla, they wanted help too, so it's a 'Catch 22'. Layla also gets frustrated when she can see her peers are able to do the work and she can't. This had a major effect on her mental health, her emotional needs and her self-esteem.

Layla had not been to school since the 5th March 2020. This was earlier than most children, because she had to have her PEG changed on the 9th March, and then she had a course of antibiotics due to her CF. So I decided not to send her to school at all after that due to the Covid-19 virus. I had an email from her hospital the following week anyway, asking me to keep her home as she was in the vulnerable category, the national shielding came into place the week after that.

I have to be truthful. I was worried about how we would be able to 'entertain' Layla for the initially suggested three months as she is a gregarious little person. Each day normally, I would be taking Layla somewhere, whether it be to the gym, swimming, arts and crafts, occupational therapy, or drama and singing classes. Well, I was proven wrong and big time! Once the panic for food, nappies and wipes had subsided due to shortage of supplies in supermarkets, we soon adjusted to this new life, quickly getting into a structured routine which we all enjoyed. And slowly, slowly, we could see the changes in Layla, she started to thrive. What I have realised is, that the behaviours Layla normally displayed on the weekends and holidays, was her dysregulated because of school. It spilt over into the weekend and holidays. During 'lockdown' having an enforced break from school and spending more time in her safe haven, meant we started to see the benefits of home-educating. Things that may mean nothing to most, but for us mean the world. For example, Layla will now eat baked beans, and not only that, she dips her chips in her baked beans!

Layla got into Lego last year, but someone had to sit and build it with her, mostly my mum. I have not got the patience. Anybody who has bought Lego sets in recent times know what I mean. The picture instruction books are designed for architects!! A few weeks ago, Layla took out her 'Lego Box' and was studying the instruction book. She came to me not long after and showed me how she built the heart shape, exactly the way it was in the book! She can also do puzzles independently now. She used to check the age on it and say I should be able to do this as it says four plus, and I am 6 but when she couldn't it knocked her self-confidence. All this helps with Layla's concentration, it builds her self-esteem and self-worth and belief in herself. All so important to be a happy person. These advances bring us such joy, we are beaming, and it shines

from the inside of us and radiates onto the outside.

Layla has started to regulate, and this meant sleeping better at night, her anxiety is quantifiably less. She has dinner now! In her 6 years and 7 months, this has never happened. She even says when she is hungry! This is a girl who used to not eat for 10 hours straight while at school and then go swimming.

Layla has learnt about different countries and she has learnt how to play tennis – a massive achievement as she struggles with co-ordination. She accepts having a ponytail when cooking or on her scooter, something that she has never done before. She has learnt how to tie her hair up herself. She can now ride her scooter. I bought one with a seat attached but removed it once she learnt to balance and co-ordinate.

Layla has also been learning to cook with her Nani. She is learning a life skill and absolutely loves it, even if 98% of what she cooks, she doesn't eat. We have started making little videos of Layla at work, 'Chef Layla's Cooking Show', and posting them on Facebook. Layla loving to cook and perform in front of the camera was the biggest surprise, but the most heart-warming thing for us, is when our friends told us how much joy the little films have bought them over the months of lockdown. Thank you for showering so much love on this little girl.

Year one had been hard for Layla as she knows she is different to her peers. Her peers can also see she is different as well. Yet the most often asked question when I mention home-educating Layla is, what about friendships and social interaction with children her age. One of the things I have learnt is that being with peers in a school setting is a negative experience for Layla. Why? Because they show her what she 'should' supposedly be achieving at her age (if we go by milestones and tick-boxes). This affects her self-esteem and self-confidence. She is also so vulnerable as she will do anything they tell her to do. For example, a girl in her class, told Layla to touch some nettles and so Layla did. When I asked Layla what happened, she said "B didn't want to sting herself so asked me to, but that's ok because we are friends". Her whole hand was blistered. Layla does not understand the concept of friendship. Layla has enough activities outside of school where she is with other children, so I am not worried.

I have also joined every group I can find on home educating, such as Home-education London, Home-education UK and home-education groups locally. Here we get so much support, resources and meet ups with other families, as well as activities arranged in the local area. One that Layla is looking forward to is 'Forest School' which is similar to the

Scouts or Guides where children learn woodland crafts and explore the environment. Once the danger of Covid-19 is manageable, I shall let Layla join in. I think friendship in a school setting is more rigid. You don't get to choose who is in your class and it's the same children every day whether they form friendships or not. In some ways that is more artificial than meeting up at an activity and seeing who they get on with and connect with.

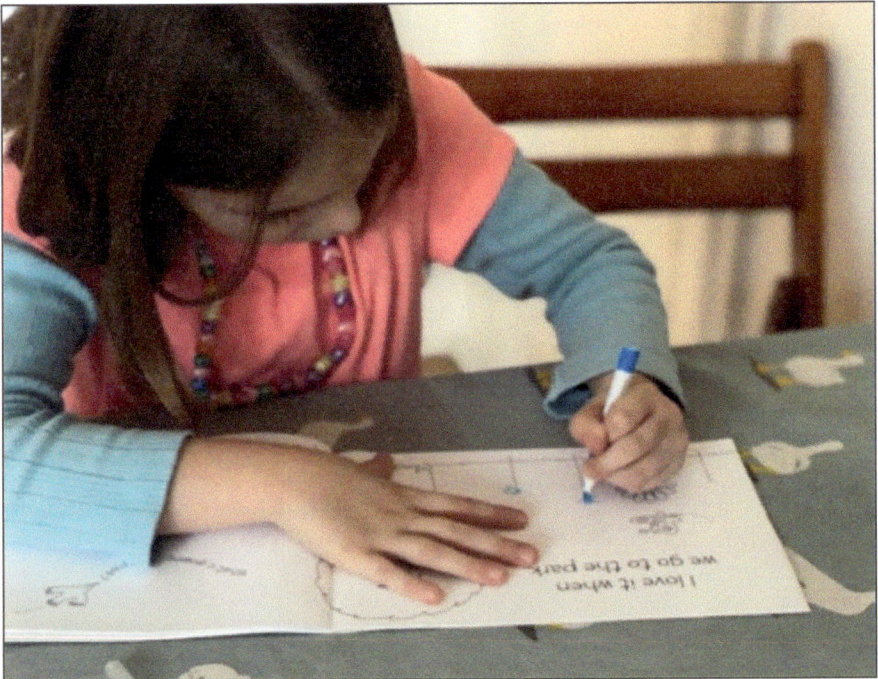

Another big factor that contributes greatly to Layla's learning, is her love of travelling and going on holidays. We travel a lot as a family, going to India, Wales and cruising once a year, as well as Butlins three times a year. In 2018 we travelled all around India, and Layla learnt about different cultures, India being one of the most diverse countries in the world. She loved this experience, watching the sun rise and the sun set, the colours and people she met. She even saw the Taj Mahal. On the cruise last year we went to Spain, France and Italy and she loved the different architecture, the dancing. The year before we went to Germany and Holland and we went to Ann Franks home. We had no family here in the UK, but now Shaun and Paul in north Wales have become family and she loves when we go and stay with them where she can be herself, having fun on the beach if the weather is dry and not too cold, seeing the sheep, doing arts and crafts and walking. She regularly remembers these experiences. We also travel most years to Chandigarh, India for a prolonged visit with extended family.

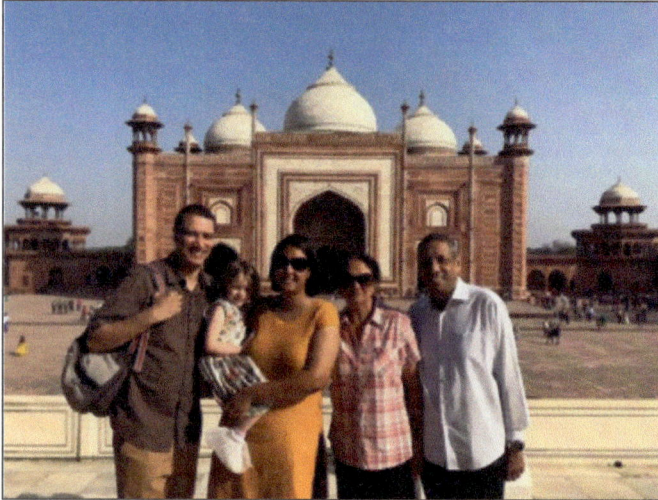

I feel that Layla has gained by learning in both the British and Asian cultures. We live day to day in a British world, while exposed to some things that are Indian, such as music, dance and food. Layla's life can only be richer for this diversity.

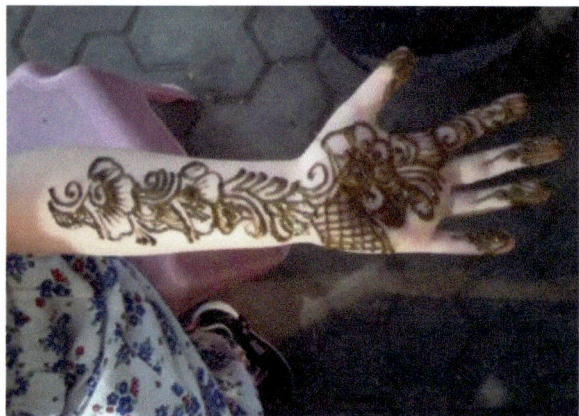

Four generations. Nani, Mridula, Shushma and Layla

I had always known school would be a worry when Layla reached secondary school age, and that I would have to think of alternatives when that day arrives, such as a therapeutic day school, but they are few and far between. Layla's consultant agreed with me that secondary school would probably be a bad idea for Layla and that a therapeutic school would be something to seriously think about, maybe even at junior school age if I felt mainstream was not for Layla. When I spoke to her again recently, she agreed to support me in home-educating, as it was in Layla's best interest. I have since spoken to two other professionals who understand Layla, and they are in agreement too.

I was petrified of home-educating Layla. What if I stuff it up? What if I don't teach the right information . . . what if I . . . ? what if . . . ? but then I remember my intentions are right, and my little girl is happy, and that's all that matters.

Chapter 12 – And so, home-education starts officially

On the 20th August 2020, I sent the official de-registration letter to the school and the local authority. I had written the letter weeks ago, but it sat in my draft inbox as I was scared, umming and aahing about sending it. Silly I know, as we had been home-educating Layla since March, yet this made it official, what if I failed Layla. There was no going back once I had sent it and the staff at the school were lovely and warm. The head teacher always had her door open for me and listened, but as it is a mainstream school it is not right for my daughter.

Whilst speaking to the psychologist the day before I sent the email, she re-affirmed that my decision was the right decision for Layla. I heard back from Layla's school acknowledging my intentions, but as of the time of writing, I am yet to hear from the local authority, they are required to write or phone me to acknowledge my home-education decision. If Layla had no special educational needs, then it would depend on the local authority just how much they got involved. An education authority may informally ask what provision the family of a child without special needs are making for the child's education, but families are not under obligation by law to reply. Interesting right! However, as Layla has special educational needs and an educational health care plan, it is required by the local authority to make sure I am providing an education that meets my daughter's needs and that I am following the EHCP. The EHCP still stands and Layla will still have an annual review in case I change my mind and want her to go back to a school, or if the local authority feel I am not providing the right education for Layla. I find it bizarre. I don't get funding, unlike her school, so you would think that the local authority would have been keener to check that the school were honouring the EHCP, not the family, who fought so hard to make sure that the content and wording of it were water-tight, with no room for ambiguity.

I was worried, I think mostly about not meeting Layla's learning needs, but it has been over a month now and we are loving it, and I now know it was in fact the best decision. My daughter is her true self again. She wants to learn, she is choosing the topics she wants to learn and she is choosing subjects she would previously have avoided as she found them hard. She now knows she can make mistakes and it's ok.

As I mentioned previously, Layla has found adding and subtracting difficult. We have been using visual objects such as Lego, food and fingers, and the other day when we were doing this, Layla actually got the concept and counted my fingers when we subtracted. It boosted her confidence so much that she asked to do Maths again the next day. A few days ago, she came to me and wanted to learn about tarantulas and had questions such as where their eyes are, how they make their webs? This was so heart-warming.

At school, Layla was being encouraged to improve faster than was natural for her. She had stopped playing with her dollies and certain toys, or colouring in worksheets and drawing, as her schoolfriends called her efforts 'babyish'. Layla now has the confidence to do these things again, and in fact, she can now colour in the line and her drawing has improved so much, probably because there is no expectation of how it *should* look and so she can draw freely. This was no fault of the other children, just another consequence of mainstream schooling.

I was very fortunate to be offered a brand-new tablet by Uncle Paul. I am old-fashioned and have not let Layla play on our phones, or go on our tablets or computers, but I know I have to one day, whilst making sure she is safe, the technology is of her generation. My mum and I recently had zoom training for the iPad, regarding how to keep Layla safe and what I need to do to block things, how to add a timer so the iPad will turn itself off after her allocated time etc. I have now downloaded an educational app based on Maths and English. Layla is allowed an hour on it a day with adult supervision, but I am lucky as she only asks for it once or twice a week and is not always on it for the full hour. This has boosted her confidence as she has to guess the words and match things and she gets excited. I will download more apps as we go along. Layla likes to listen to

music, and I introduced the MP3 player last year as a strategy when she needed to regulate.

I have also found another strategy that has helped Layla and that is mindfulness colour sheets. Layla chooses what she wants to colour in, but the concentration when she tries to stay in the lines is good for her fine motor skills and builds up her endurance. It's also good for the small muscles in her hands whilst it helps her endurance when writing. The colouring keeps her focused which in turn regulates her.

As I've mentioned before, Layla fell in love with cooking during the shielding, and took such interest in it, that my mum started adapting 'lessons' for her, such as having smaller bowls, weighing the ingredients in halves (so instead of weighing 8oz of flour, mum will get Layla to weigh 4oz and then another 4oz), whilst she can tip the flour in the bowls and stir the ingredients independently. Though she still needs assistance with some parts of the process, her skills are growing daily. Her baking repertoire includes pizzas, pasties, Bakewell tarts and lots of fairy cakes. My mum has been buying equipment and utensils for Layla, so she has her own things. Cooking day takes a lot of planning, making sure she has all the ingredients and enough time as mum goes at Layla's pace, and adapts everything so that Layla can do it independently wherever possible. During her cooking lessons, Layla has learnt the names of different spices, exotic vegetables and herbs, which country they come from and how they grow, as well as useful Maths using the weighing scale. But the most important thing is she loves it!

As long as the weather is ok (the cold damp weather affects Layla's lungs), Layla chooses to either go on her bike or scooter daily. We do this first thing in the morning, usually at 7am, after Layla has had a shower and breakfast, so she burns off the energy first thing to clear her mind and regulate. It also keeps her lungs clear, builds up her muscle tone and helps her co-ordinate. I am also teaching her to know or feel when her body is tired and to then slow down or rest. I am also trying to teach her, that her body may be thirsty or hungry after exercise so I will give a 60ml flush or water and a piece of fruit. Sometimes Layla will say herself she is thirsty or hungry. We have also been learning whilst we are out and about, such diverse things as, how and why we can blow clouds in cold air, about bees and sunflowers. Layla lets her imagination run wild. In our road, she's found something in the tarmac which she has named, 'Gandhi's stick!'

'Gandhi's stick!'

Another new thing that Layla got into during shielding, is the playstation. She first saw one in the hospital she goes to and would watch other children play or try and play herself. We had a PlayStation 4 sitting gathering dust, which Layla asked if she could play with. We bought two games and she taught herself to play with Uncle Nitin supervising. She doesn't play for long, sometimes 20 minutes a day, sometimes an hour a day or sometimes none. It builds her confidence as she self-explores and goes up through the levels, losing many times, but knowing this is ok. Another friend, John, a music teacher, has set up a music account for Layla so she can learn to sing and play. John uploads appropriate materials for Layla to use. She loves this and is learning ABBA music at the moment.

Sometimes home-education can be overwhelming, there is so much advice out there and paths to explore that I can get too zoned into it, and then confused about what to teach Layla next. I have to take a step back and remind myself that it has to be something that will engage Layla, as that's how she will learn, and that I can't teach her *everything*.

Layla loves acting, singing and dancing and I have been thinking of getting her to do her own nativity play for Christmas as Mary or singing some Christmas carols while I film it, but I have a feeling I am being too ambitious. Time will tell.

It is lovely when things happen unexpectedly, especially when Layla comes to me to say what she wants to learn. Nani was recycling the egg carton, when Layla took it and said to me, mummy we can make the enormous crocodile (a few days earlier we had learned about Roald Dahl as it was Roald Dahl day.) It was a lot of fun making the crocodile.

I have decided to make a display board so that Layla can display her artwork or any piece of work as and when she wants to, changing it each term or when she wishes to. Hopefully this will reinforce how much she has achieved.

I'm learning to slow down and not to be disheartened if I don't get to do things I had planned with Layla on a certain day. I like to be organised and on top of things, but I can't control home-education, home-education controls me. Why? Because it's a home, and home consists of children, housework, working from home, and so I have to go with the flow. I'm learning to accept this as time goes by and to not beat myself up about it or see it as failing Layla.

Making our own resources has been fun, one being a daily calendar for Layla to change the day, month and year. This will help her understand how dates work, the seasons, the weather (looking outside to see if she can go on her scooter). Mostly, I want Layla to learn life skills that are important for her to be independent, as and where possible, especially when none of us are around.

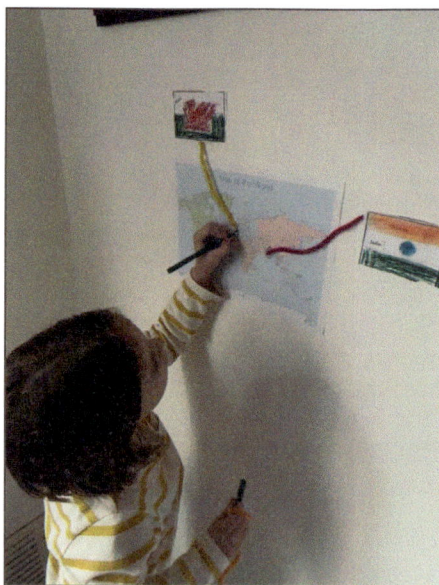

The only down-side so far is, when Layla does step out of her haven, she becomes so stimulated by the environment that she becomes dysregulated, to the point where she is likely to explode. It reminds me how she was when she went to school. With time though, we will hopefully find strategies that will help Layla interact with the outside world, and once things start to open again after Covid-19, Layla will, with time, get used to the busy environment again, and if she doesn't, that's ok too as she has us to support her with it.

Recently Layla was diagnosed with autism and ADHD. Having the autism diagnosis means that the choice of schools available for her widens, and

Layla could go to a nurturing school in the future, but for now I am happy to follow the home-education option.

We have all learnt so much during shielding. I am amazed how much it has taught me, and it all started when I decided to keep a scrapbook of our memories, during the initial four and half month period of 'lockdown'. This is for Layla to keep, as a piece of history and to remind her of this period of great change (she also really enjoyed making it). It showed me that Layla can learn at home from us and enjoy it. Layla trusts us and this is how she will learn to be herself.

I am teaching her that practice makes progress, not perfection, as nothing in this life is perfect. I love my child and I want her to become everything she is capable of. It's not *just* about Layla not coping well in the school environment, it's about giving Layla the foundation to thrive for the rest of her life.

Paraphrasing Chris Britten, headteacher of 'Ysgol Y Deri', Britain's largest special education school . . . 'Society teaches and shows my daughter what she can't do. I teach and show her what she can do'.

Useful links . . .

Health and support organizations . . .

www.adoptionuk.org – Adoption UK for every adoptive family

www.childmind.org/article/what-to-do-and-not-do-when-children-are-anxious/ - Child Mind Institute

www.cysticfibrosis.org.uk – Cystic Fibrosis Trust

www.danielhughes.org - Dyadic Developmental Psychotherapy, Attachment Focused Treatment for Childhood Trauma & Abuse

www.fasdnetwork.org/resources.html - FASD Network UK

www.mencap.org.uk – 'The voice of learning disability'

www.nhsaaa.net/media/5701/alcohol-pregnancy-a5-booklet-final.pdf - NHS Alcohol and pregnancy

www.nationalfasd.org.uk – National organisation for FASD

www.pac-uk.org – Specialist therapy, advice, support, counselling and training for all affected by adoption and permanency

www.rcpsych.ac.uk/mental-health/parents-and-young-people/information-for-parents-and-carers/the-child-with-general-learning-disability-for-parents-and-carers - Royal College of Psychiatrists www.researchautism.org/its-not-picky-eating-5-strategies-for-sensory-food-sensitivities - Organisation for Autism Research

www.specialneedsguide.co.uk/news/a-parents-guide-to-understanding-your-childs-spiky-learning-profile

Home education resources . . .

www.barrycarpentereducation.com/tag/fasd/ - International Educational consultant

www.beaconschoolsupport.co.uk/newsletters/self-regulation-the-key-to-helping-others - Help for schools, teachers and families when behaviour gets in the way of success

www.educationandadoption.wordpress.com/author/stuartguestblog/ - Schools, Education and Adoption